OLYMPIC LEGENDS

BOXING

BY SHANE FREDERICK

CREATIVE ✻ EDUCATION

BOXING

CONTENTS

INTRODUCTION

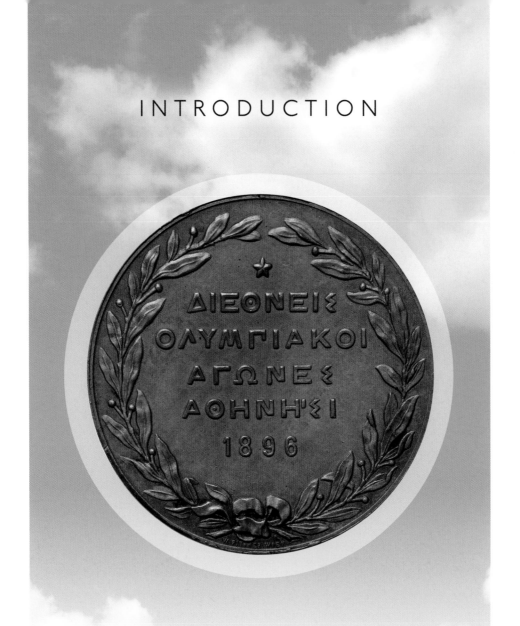

Throughout human history, people have always sought to challenge themselves, to compete against others, and to discover the limits of their capabilities. Such desires can turn destructive, leading to war. But the ancient Greeks also recognized the good in these human traits, and it was because of them that the Olympic Games—featuring running races, jumping contests, throwing competitions, and wrestling and boxing matches—began more than 2,700 years ago. The ancient Olympics ended in A.D. 393, but the Games were revived in 1896 in hopes of promoting world peace through sports. Fittingly, the first "modern" Olympics were held in Athens, Greece, but they moved around the world every four years after that. In 2009, it was announced that the Games would be held in South America for the first time, going to Rio de Janeiro, Brazil, in 2016.

Every 1896 Olympian received a medal reading "International Olympic Games, Athens 1896"

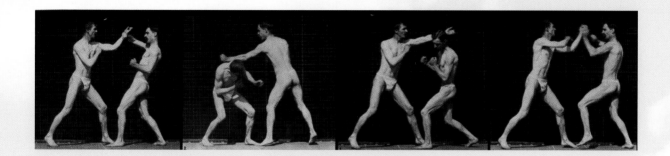

One of the Greeks' original sports, boxing puts two fighters into a ring—a large, square mat surrounded by ropes—and each tries to score points by landing punches to the other's head or body. Judges watch the bouts and award points, and the boxer with the most points wins the match. Fighters can also win by knocking out their opponents (KO) or by displaying such dominance that the referee must stop the contest to protect the beaten fighter—a technical knockout (TKO). The sport has evolved since it was introduced to the modern Olympics in 1904. In 1984, Olympic boxers were required for the first time to wear protective headgear, and in 2012 in London, England, women's boxing was to be part of the Games for the first time.

The Olympics have introduced the world to some of the greatest boxers in history. Cassius Clay (Muhammad Ali), Joe Frazier, George Foreman, and "Sugar" Ray Leonard all won gold medals before going on to become professional champions. Boxing has also been one of the most controversial sports in the Games, with incidents of biting, illegal punches, and corrupt judges having changed the outcome of some matches, or bouts. However, the grace with which some of those wronged fighters handled their heartbreaks and losses has helped make boxing one of the most inspirational sports on the Olympic stage.

Boxing is an ancient form of competition pure in its simplicity: two people fight with nothing but fists

ATHENS, GREECE	PARIS, FRANCE	ST. LOUIS, MISSOURI	LONDON, ENGLAND	STOCKHOLM, SWEDEN	ANTWERP, BELGIUM	PARIS, FRANCE	AMSTERDAM, NETHERLANDS	LOS ANGELES, CALIFORNIA	BERLIN, GERMANY	LONDON, ENGLAND	HELSINKI, FINLAND	MELBOURNE, AUSTRALIA	ROME, ITALY	TOKYO, JAPAN	MEXICO CITY, MEXICO	MUNICH, WEST GERMANY	MONTRÉAL, QUEBEC	MOSCOW, SOVIET UNION	LOS ANGELES, CALIFORNIA	SEOUL, SOUTH KOREA	BARCELONA, SPAIN	ATLANTA, GEORGIA	SYDNEY, AUSTRALIA	ATHENS, GREECE	BEIJING, CHINA	LONDON, ENGLAND
1896	1900	1904	1908	1912	1920	1924	1928	1932	1936	1948	1952	1956	1960	1964	1968	1972	1976	1980	1984	1988	1992	1996	2000	2004	2008	2012

CAPTAIN KIRK

OLIVER KIRK   UNITED STATES   WEIGHT CLASSES: BANTAMWEIGHT, FEATHERWEIGHT

OLYMPIC COMPETITION: 1904

When the modern Olympics were reintroduced in 1896, they did not include a boxing competition, even though it was an event in the ancient Greeks' original Games. Although it was a popular sport at the time, organizers of the 1896 Olympics called it "ungentlemanly, dangerous, and practiced by

No boxer ever had a shorter road to Olympic gold than Oliver Kirk, who won two medals with two fights

6

the dregs of the population." Boxing was kept out of the 1900 Olympics in Paris, France, too, before finally being added in 1904 in St. Louis, Missouri.

The first boxing competition wasn't perfect. Before the advent of air travel, it was a long journey for people from other countries to get to the middle of the United States. So few athletes went to St. Louis that all the boxers were Americans. Some of the sport's seven weight classes had only two fighters facing off for the gold medal. Only two classes had more than three boxers. The competition went down in history, though, because it featured something that almost certainly will never be accomplished again in Olympic boxing.

St. Louis resident Oliver Kirk was in one of the two-man divisions. Fighting at bantamweight, a class for men weighing up to 115 pounds, Kirk defeated his only competition, George Finnegan, by way of TKO, with the referee stopping the bout in the final round.

Boxing weight classes were created in the interests of safe and fair competition. However, the sport's rules allow fighters to move up into a heavier weight class, if they think they can compete against bigger boxers. Like the bantamweight division, the 125-pound featherweight class also had just two entrants, Frank Haller and Fred Gilmore, in 1904. The crowd at the Washington University gymnasium clamored for the 20-year-old Kirk to take on the winner of that match for the gold. Kirk was game, and Olympic officials agreed to it. After Haller defeated Gilmore, he stepped back into the ring against Kirk. The smaller Kirk won the bout by decision and earned a place in the history books as the only boxer in Olympic history to win two gold medals in separate weight classes in the same Games.

Boxing gloves were developed both to protect fighters' hands and to reduce the likelihood of facial cuts

ATHENS, GREECE | PARIS, FRANCE | ST. LOUIS, MISSOURI | LONDON, ENGLAND | STOCKHOLM, SWEDEN | ANTWERP, BELGIUM | PARIS, FRANCE | AMSTERDAM, NETHERLANDS | LOS ANGELES, CALIFORNIA | BERLIN, GERMANY | LONDON, ENGLAND | HELSINKI, FINLAND | MELBOURNE, AUSTRALIA | ROME, ITALY | TOKYO, JAPAN | MEXICO CITY, MEXICO | MUNICH, WEST GERMANY | MONTREAL, QUEBEC | MOSCOW, SOVIET UNION | LOS ANGELES, CALIFORNIA | SEOUL, SOUTH KOREA | BARCELONA, SPAIN | ATLANTA, GEORGIA | SYDNEY, AUSTRALIA | ATHENS, GREECE | BEIJING, CHINA | LONDON, ENGLAND

1896 | 1900 | 1904 | 1908 | 1912 | 1920 | 1924 | 1928 | 1932 | 1936 | 1948 | 1952 | 1956 | 1960 | 1964 | 1968 | 1972 | 1976 | 1980 | 1984 | 1988 | 1992 | 1996 | 2000 | 2004 | 2008 | 2012

BITING AND FIGHTING

1924 PARIS, FRANCE

Henry William "Harry" Mallin was considered one of the greatest amateur boxers to come out of Great Britain. The Englishman, who never turned professional (he was a London policeman), never lost in more than 300 career bouts. He won the gold medal in the middleweight division in the 1920 Olympics in Antwerp, Belgium, and became the first Olympic boxer to defend his title by taking the

After his fighting days, Harry Mallin went on to manage Britain's boxing team in the 1936 Olympics

8

gold at the 1924 Games in Paris, France. "He was untouchable in the boxing ring," *The Times* newspaper of London wrote of Mallin, "and the only way that he was going to lose was at the hands of a cheat." Make that the *teeth* of a cheat.

After easily winning his first two matches in Paris, Mallin faced Frenchman and crowd-favorite Roger Brousse in the quarterfinals. As Mallin tried to score points with his punches, he felt a pain on his arm. Brousse was biting him! Mallin pulled his arm away, but in the next round, Brousse chomped down on his chest as he landed a blow to Mallin's chin.

When the final bell rang, Mallin took off his vest, went to the referee, and showed him the teeth marks on his chest. But when the final decision was announced, officials declared Brousse to be the winner, meaning Mallin had lost his first fight in 14 years of boxing. Mallin protested the decision, and during a late-night hearing, another boxer said that Brousse had bitten him, too. Eventually, officials ruled for Mallin and disqualified Brousse.

The French spectators were outraged by the decision. Fights broke out in the stands, and fans carried Brousse around the arena on their shoulders before Mallin's next bout. They even tried to bring Brousse into the ring as Mallin and his semifinal opponent, Belgium's Joseph Beecken, watched and waited. Mallin defeated Beecken in a decision and then went on to beat his fellow countryman, John Elliot, in the gold-medal match.

That wasn't the only controversial decision in Mallin's Olympic career. During the 1920 Games, he had defeated American Sam Lagonia after Lagonia was disqualified for constant holding. The U.S. team was furious with the decision, but Mallin went on to take the gold medal, defeating powerful Canadian Art Prud'homme in the final.

ATHENS, GREECE
PARIS, FRANCE
ST. LOUIS, MISSOURI
LONDON, ENGLAND
STOCKHOLM, SWEDEN
ANTWERP, BELGIUM
PARIS, FRANCE
AMSTERDAM, NETHERLANDS
LOS ANGELES, CALIFORNIA
BERLIN, GERMANY
LONDON, ENGLAND
HELSINKI, FINLAND
MELBOURNE, AUSTRALIA
ROME, ITALY
TOKYO, JAPAN
MEXICO CITY, MEXICO
MUNICH, WEST GERMANY
MONTREAL, QUEBEC
MOSCOW, SOVIET UNION
LOS ANGELES, CALIFORNIA
SEOUL, SOUTH KOREA
BARCELONA, SPAIN
ATLANTA, GEORGIA
SYDNEY, AUSTRALIA
ATHENS, GREECE
BEIJING, CHINA
LONDON, ENGLAND

1896 1900 1904 1908 1912 1920 1924 1928 1932 **1936** 1948 1952 1956 1960 1964 1968 1972 1976 1980 1984 1988 1992 1996 2000 2004 2008 2012

THE MAN WHO ATE TOO MUCH

1936 BERLIN, GERMANY

While lighter boxers are allowed to move up a weight class if they so choose, heavier boxers cannot move down. They must remain within the limits of their weight class throughout the Olympics.

Staying at or below the 135-pound limit for the lightweight division was difficult for South African boxer Thomas Hamilton-Brown going into the 1936 Olympics in Berlin, Germany. But

Weigh-ins usually occur the day before a match, giving boxers the chance to add weight before fighting

he made weight for his first bout against Carlos Lillo of Chile. After the match ended, the three judges turned in their scores, and it was announced that Lillo won by split decision: two judges picked Lillo as the winner, and one voted for Hamilton-Brown.

The South African was depressed, his dreams of winning an Olympic medal dashed. He decided that the way to make himself feel better was to eat. So he went on a binge, eating and eating and eating. That turned out to be a big mistake. While Hamilton-Brown was eating, Olympic officials double-checked the scores. It turned out that one of the judges erred and reversed his scores. He meant to have Hamilton-Brown as the winner, not Lillo.

Word quickly reached Hamilton-Brown that he had actually won and was scheduled to fight again in the second round of the tournament. The only problem was that he had gained five pounds from eating so much. The night before the next weigh-in, he did everything he could to sweat off the extra pounds quickly, from spending hours in a steam room or sauna, to jogging or exercising in heavy clothes, to denying himself water. It was no use. When Hamilton-Brown stepped on the scale, he was still too heavy to make weight in his class. He was disqualified.

Officials allowed the original decision to stand, and Lillo won his next bout before losing to the eventual silver medalist, Nikolai Stepulov of Estonia, in the quarterfinals. Meanwhile, Thomas Hamilton-Brown became famous for making one of the biggest blunders in Olympic history.

As of 2012, men's Olympic boxing featured 10 weight classes

flyweight	up to 112 pounds
bantamweight	up to 119
featherweight	up to 126
lightweight	up to 132
light-welterweight	up to 141
welterweight	up to 152
middleweight	up to 165
light-heavyweight	up to 179
heavyweight	up to 201
super-heavyweight	more than 201

ATHENS, GREECE	PARIS, FRANCE	ST. LOUIS, MISSOURI	LONDON, ENGLAND	STOCKHOLM, SWEDEN	ANTWERP, BELGIUM	PARIS, FRANCE	AMSTERDAM, NETHERLANDS	LOS ANGELES, CALIFORNIA	BERLIN, GERMANY	LONDON, ENGLAND	HELSINKI, FINLAND	MELBOURNE, AUSTRALIA	ROME, ITALY	TOKYO, JAPAN	MEXICO CITY, MEXICO	MUNICH, WEST GERMANY	MONTREAL, QUEBEC	MOSCOW, SOVIET UNION	LOS ANGELES, CALIFORNIA	SEOUL, SOUTH KOREA	BARCELONA, SPAIN	ATLANTA, GEORGIA	SYDNEY, AUSTRALIA	ATHENS, GREECE	BEIJING, CHINA	LONDON, ENGLAND
1896	1900	1904	1908	1912	1920	1924	1928	1932	1936	1948	1952	1956	1960	1964	1968	1972	1976	1980	1984	1988	1992	1996	2000	2004	2008	2012

BIG PAPP

LÁSZLÓ PAPP HUNGARY WEIGHT CLASSES: MIDDLEWEIGHT, LIGHT-MIDDLEWEIGHT

OLYMPIC COMPETITIONS: 1948, 1952, 1956

Lászó Papp wanted to earn money as a boxer. But for most of his career, he was not allowed to become a professional fighter. The **communist** government in Hungary wouldn't allow its athletes to turn pro and travel the world on their own to compete. They had to remain amateurs and represent

László Papp never lost an Olympic fight, winning with seven decisions, four KOs, and two TKOs

their country in international competition. But that didn't mean those athletes couldn't achieve fame.

In the 1940s and '50s, Papp proved that he was one of the best boxers in the world, compiling an amateur record of 288 wins and 12 losses. More significantly, he became the first Olympic athlete to win three gold medals in boxing. He captured the middleweight title in 1948 in London, England, and the light-middleweight gold in 1952 in Helsinki, Finland, and again in 1956 in Melbourne, Australia.

Papp was known for his phenomenal footwork in the ring. But he also fought with an unorthodox style. He was right-handed but frequently fought as a southpaw, catching his opponents off-guard with a powerful left hook. In London, Papp worked his way through a talented middleweight division before defeating the home favorite, Englishman Johnny Wright, in the championship bout. Hungary's coach, Bela Keri, promised that if both Papp and bantamweight Tibor Csík won gold medals, he'd jump into a swimming pool with all his clothes on. Csík emerged as champion, too, and Keri lived up to his promise. Papp defeated Theunis van Schalkwyk of South Africa for the gold in Helsinki. And for his last gold medal, Papp defeated an up-and-coming fighter from the U.S. named Jose Torres. Torres would later win the world light-heavyweight title as a professional.

After his success in Melbourne, Papp finally received permission to fight professionally, ending his golden winning streak. "I think I could have won a fourth gold had I stayed in amateur boxing," Papp said, "but I wanted to make some money." Since 1956, only two other boxers have matched Papp's feat of winning three gold medals.

ATHENS, GREECE 1896
PARIS, FRANCE 1900
ST. LOUIS, MISSOURI 1904
LONDON, ENGLAND 1908
STOCKHOLM, SWEDEN 1912
ANTWERP, BELGIUM 1920
PARIS, FRANCE 1924
AMSTERDAM, NETHERLANDS 1928
LOS ANGELES, CALIFORNIA 1932
BERLIN, GERMANY 1936
LONDON, ENGLAND 1948
HELSINKI, FINLAND 1952
MELBOURNE, AUSTRALIA 1956
ROME, ITALY 1960
TOKYO, JAPAN 1964
MEXICO CITY, MEXICO 1968
MUNICH, WEST GERMANY 1972
MONTREAL, QUEBEC 1976
MOSCOW, SOVIET UNION 1980
LOS ANGELES, CALIFORNIA 1984
SEOUL, SOUTH KOREA 1988
BARCELONA, SPAIN 1992
ATLANTA, GEORGIA 1996
SYDNEY, AUSTRALIA 2000
ATHENS, GREECE 2004
BEIJING, CHINA 2008
LONDON, ENGLAND 2012

YOUNG GUNS

1952 HELSINKI, FINLAND

During the 1948 Olympics in London, England, the U.S. won just one boxing medal, a silver. Four years later in Helsinki, Finland, however, the Americans dominated the ring. They won 5 gold medals in 10 events, and they did it with youth.

Floyd Patterson (left) was a delinquent as a youth but became known as one of boxing's true gentlemen

The youngest fighter in the group was a 17-year-old middleweight named Floyd Patterson. Patterson, who later became the heavyweight champion of the world as a professional, packed a powerful punch in the Olympics. He scored two first-round knockouts on his way to the gold. That included some quick work against Romania's Vasile Tita in the gold-medal bout. A right uppercut to the chin knocked Tita to the mat, and the fight was over in just 74 seconds. A fan complained to Patterson, "I like to see you fight, but you never fight long enough."

While Patterson was the most famous of the American fighters, he wasn't the only one to do great things in Helsinki. Eighteen-year-old Nate Brooks won the flyweight title with a unanimous decision over Germany's Edgar Basel. The oldest champ of the group, 27-year-old light-heavyweight Norvel Lee, likewise out-pointed Argentina's Antonio Pacenza. Lee, a longtime amateur boxing star and Patterson's Olympic sparring partner, also won the Val Barker Trophy as the Olympics' best overall boxer, regardless of weight class.

In the heavyweight division, 22-year-old Ed Sanders won the gold by beating Sweden's Ingemar Johansson. Johansson, a future professional champion (he would later knock out Patterson to win the title), was disqualified in the finals for trying to run away from the hard-punching Sanders. "Big Ed" had knocked out his first two opponents and won in the semifinals when the referee stopped the fight in the second round. Some critics thought Johansson was afraid, calling him "the fleeing rat" and "a plain coward." The Swede argued in vain that he was not avoiding Sanders but rather was trying to tire him out so that he could go after him in the third and final round.

While the U.S. would produce some great champions after 1952, it would be 24 years before the country would win 5 boxing gold medals in a single Olympics again.

Nate Brooks (opposite, left) won decisions in all five of his Olympic fights in 1952 en route to gold

ATHENS, GREECE	PARIS, FRANCE	ST. LOUIS, MISSOURI	LONDON, ENGLAND	STOCKHOLM, SWEDEN	ANTWERP, BELGIUM	PARIS, FRANCE	AMSTERDAM, NETHERLANDS	LOS ANGELES, CALIFORNIA	BERLIN, GERMANY	LONDON, ENGLAND	HELSINKI, FINLAND	MELBOURNE, AUSTRALIA	ROME, ITALY	TOKYO, JAPAN	MEXICO CITY, MEXICO	MUNICH, WEST GERMANY	MONTREAL, QUEBEC	MOSCOW, SOVIET UNION	LOS ANGELES, CALIFORNIA	SEOUL, SOUTH KOREA	BARCELONA, SPAIN	ATLANTA, GEORGIA	SYDNEY, AUSTRALIA	ATHENS, GREECE	BEIJING, CHINA	LONDON, ENGLAND
1896	1900	1904	1908	1912	1920	1924	1928	1932	1936	1948	1952	1956	**1960**	1964	1968	1972	1976	1980	1984	1988	1992	1996	2000	2004	2008	2012

BEFORE ALI

CASSIUS CLAY UNITED STATES WEIGHT CLASS: LIGHT-HEAVYWEIGHT

OLYMPIC COMPETITION: 1960

Before he changed his name to Muhammad Ali, before he became heavyweight champion of the world, before he became one of the most recognizable people on Earth, Cassius Clay was an 18-year-old boxer hoping to win Olympic gold. A native of Louisville, Kentucky, Clay arrived at the 1960 games in Rome, Italy,

By winning Olympic gold, Cassius Clay began his transformation into the world's most famous athlete

ready to take on the Games' light-heavyweight division—the weight class considered the most talent-rich at the Olympics.

Despite his youth, Clay wasn't intimidated by the roster of boxers he was about to face. He bragged about his skills and called himself "the greatest of all time." He spent the Games walking around Rome, mingling with athletes and **ambassadors** alike, and became a celebrity himself.

Clay was also a superstar in the ring. He showed off his supreme footwork by dancing and skipping around the ring, sneaking in a **jab** or two whenever he could. In his first match in Rome, Clay defeated Belgium's Yvon Becot by TKO in the second round. In the quarterfinals, Clay got a unanimous decision from the judges in a win over Gennady Shatkov of the Soviet Union. "I shook Clay's hand," said Shatkov, who had been a gold medalist as a middleweight four years earlier in Melbourne, Australia. "It was no disgrace to lose to a boxer like that."

Clay beat Tony Madigan of Australia on points in the semifinals but faced his toughest challenge last. Zbigniew Pietrzykowski (*zuh-BIN-yev pee-EH-treh-KOW-skee*) of Poland was a tall, experienced southpaw and the reigning European champion. He had won a bronze medal in Melbourne and would win another bronze in 1964 in Tokyo, Japan. Clay's **corner** told him that he "had to go all out to win."

Pietrzykowski gave Clay trouble in the first two rounds, and it was a close fight going into the final round. That's when Clay stopped dancing and started punching, unleashing **combinations** of blows that bloodied the Pole's nose and mouth. *Ring* magazine wrote: "Clay's last-round assault on Pietrzykowski was the outstanding hitting of the tournament." Clay didn't score a knockout in the final round, but he did earn a unanimous decision. British boxer Dick McTaggart, a bronze medalist in Rome, watched the match and said, "Clay had me in awe. I was completely mesmerized. I'd been around a few years and had seen some magnificent amateurs. But never before, nor since, have I seen anyone with that level of speed and skill."

Clay began a 20-year pro career shortly after the Olympics and eventually changed his name after converting to the religion of Islam. But he had one more Olympic moment remaining. In 1996 in Atlanta, Georgia, Muhammad Ali returned to the Olympics and lit the torch during the Opening Ceremonies to officially kick off the Games.

ATHENS, GREECE	PARIS, FRANCE	ST. LOUIS, MISSOURI	LONDON, ENGLAND	STOCKHOLM, SWEDEN	ANTWERP, BELGIUM	PARIS, FRANCE	AMSTERDAM, NETHERLANDS	LOS ANGELES, CALIFORNIA	BERLIN, GERMANY	LONDON, ENGLAND	HELSINKI, FINLAND	MELBOURNE, AUSTRALIA	ROME, ITALY	TOKYO, JAPAN	MEXICO CITY, MEXICO	MUNICH, WEST GERMANY	MONTREAL, QUEBEC	MOSCOW, SOVIET UNION	LOS ANGELES, CALIFORNIA	SEOUL, SOUTH KOREA	BARCELONA, SPAIN	ATLANTA, GEORGIA	SYDNEY, AUSTRALIA	ATHENS, GREECE	BEIJING, CHINA	LONDON, ENGLAND
1896	1900	1904	1908	1912	1920	1924	1928	1932	1936	1948	1952	1956	1960	1964	1968	1972	1976	1980	1984	1988	1992	1996	2000	2004	2008	2012

FIGHTING ONE-HANDED

1964   TOKYO, JAPAN

Joe Frazier wasn't supposed to fight in the 1964 Olympics. Before the Games began in Tokyo, Japan, Buster Mathis defeated Frazier in the Olympic Trials, the competition used to determine which fighters would represent the U.S. in the Games. Only one boxer from each weight class got to move on. But while training for the Olympics, Mathis broke his thumb and was forced to withdraw from the competition

Joe Frazier, later a bitter rival of Muhammad Ali's, fought with an aggressive, crouching style

before it began. Frazier, as the alternate, was chosen to take Mathis's place in the ring.

In Tokyo, Frazier cruised through the competition, winning each of his first three matches by TKO. In the last of those bouts, a semifinal match with the Soviet Union's Vadim Yemelyanov that put him into the gold-medal match, "Smokin' Joe" suffered an injury just like Mathis's: He broke his left thumb.

Frazier feared he wouldn't be able to fight in the finals two days later. If Olympic officials found out about his thumb, he knew they might make him drop out of the event for his own safety. So he kept quiet about the injury, determined to tough it out and go for the gold. "Although my thumb was throbbing with pain, I didn't say a word about it to the coaches or my teammates," Frazier later admitted.

Later, when he turned professional and became the heavyweight champion of the

world, Frazier's best punch was a mighty left hook. But in the Olympic gold-medal bout against Hans Huber of West Germany, he barely had use of that hand. He threw most of his punches with his right, basically fighting one-handed in the biggest match of his life up to that time. "With the limitations of my left hand, it wasn't an easy fight," he said. "But I went out there acting like I wanted to win."

When the match was over, 3 of the judges voted for the 20-year-old Frazier, and 2 voted for Huber, giving Smokin' Joe the gold medal by the slimmest of margins. Frazier's medal was the only gold for the U.S. boxing team in 1964.

> **"With the limitations of my left hand, it wasn't an easy fight. But I went out there acting like I wanted to win."** – *Joe Frazier*

ATHENS, GREECE	PARIS, FRANCE	ST. LOUIS, MISSOURI	LONDON, ENGLAND	STOCKHOLM, SWEDEN	ANTWERP, BELGIUM	PARIS, FRANCE	AMSTERDAM, NETHERLANDS	LOS ANGELES, CALIFORNIA	BERLIN, GERMANY	LONDON, ENGLAND	HELSINKI, FINLAND	MELBOURNE, AUSTRALIA	ROME, ITALY	TOKYO, JAPAN	MEXICO CITY, MEXICO	MUNICH, WEST GERMANY	MONTREAL, QUEBEC	MOSCOW, SOVIET UNION	LOS ANGELES, CALIFORNIA	SEOUL, SOUTH KOREA	BARCELONA, SPAIN	ATLANTA, GEORGIA	SYDNEY, AUSTRALIA	ATHENS, GREECE	BEIJING, CHINA	LONDON, ENGLAND
1896	1900	1904	1908	1912	1920	1924	1928	1932	1936	1948	1952	1956	1960	1964	1968	1972	1976	1980	1984	1988	1992	1996	2000	2004	2008	2012

BIG MAN, LITTLE FLAG

1968 MEXICO CITY, MEXICO

George Foreman achieved fame and fortune by twice becoming the heavyweight champion of the world—the second time when he was 45 years old—and, later, by selling his own brand of electric grills. But in 1968, few people in America knew his name. He was 19 years old and had been boxing

George Foreman, pictured here at age 23, earned a reputation as one of the hardest punchers in history

23

for only a year and a half, fighting in just 20 amateur bouts, by the time the Olympics began that October in Mexico City, Mexico.

Despite his inexperience, the 6-foot-4 and 218-pound heavyweight from Houston, Texas, was strong and packed a powerful punch. "Big George" knew the art of boxing, too, and he didn't go to Mexico planning to knock out every opponent in the single-elimination tournament. He knew that judges awarded points when any punch connected, no matter how hard it landed. "I'm not concentrating on slugging so much," he told reporters. "International rules respect thinking. They represent a less brutal sport."

Foreman's Olympic opponents probably thought he was plenty brutal. After winning his first match on points, Big George knocked out his next two foes before facing the Soviet Union's

> **"It was about identity. An American— that's who I was. I was waving the flag as much for myself as my country."** – *George Foreman*

Jonas Cepulis in the gold-medal bout. Cepulis was 10 years older, but Foreman had 3 inches and 15 pounds on his veteran opponent.

Early in the fight, Foreman bloodied Cepulis's nose with a left jab. Knowing he didn't have to deliver big punches, the American kept throwing jab after jab, landing as many as 200 in the first 2 rounds before the referee stopped the fight. To the surprise of many, Foreman had won the gold medal.

After the match, Foreman waved a tiny American flag. He took it to each side of the ring and bowed to the crowd. Some other black American athletes used their medal-winning performances that year to protest racial inequality in the U.S. But Foreman said his decision to wave the flag was not a reaction to those views. "It was about identity," he said. "An American—that's who I was. I was waving the flag as much for myself as my country."

Foreman's quiet demonstration of patriotism in the 1968 Games earned him many new American fans

ATHENS, GREECE 1896
PARIS, FRANCE 1900
ST. LOUIS, MISSOURI 1904
LONDON, ENGLAND 1908
STOCKHOLM, SWEDEN 1912
ANTWERP, BELGIUM 1920
PARIS, FRANCE 1924
AMSTERDAM, NETHERLANDS 1928
LOS ANGELES, CALIFORNIA 1932
BERLIN, GERMANY 1936
LONDON, ENGLAND 1948
HELSINKI, FINLAND 1952
MELBOURNE, AUSTRALIA 1956
ROME, ITALY 1960
TOKYO, JAPAN 1964
MEXICO CITY, MEXICO 1968
MUNICH, WEST GERMANY 1972
MONTREAL, QUEBEC 1976
MOSCOW, SOVIET UNION 1980
LOS ANGELES, CALIFORNIA 1984
SEOUL, SOUTH KOREA 1988
BARCELONA, SPAIN 1992
ATLANTA, GEORGIA 1996
SYDNEY, AUSTRALIA 2000
ATHENS, GREECE 2004
BEIJING, CHINA 2008
LONDON, ENGLAND 2012

STEVENSON'S STAGE

TEÓFILO STEVENSON CUBA WEIGHT CLASS: HEAVYWEIGHT

OLYMPIC COMPETITIONS: 1972, 1976, 1980

After winning their gold medals, Cassius Clay, Joe Frazier, and George Foreman all became professional boxers. Over the years, the three men fought each other, and each eventually became the heavyweight champion of the world. But the 1972 heavyweight gold medalist, Cuba's Teófilo

Teófilo Stevenson (pictured, opposite, in the 1980 gold-medal match) scored points with his long reach

Stevenson, remained an amateur fighter throughout his career and is considered the greatest heavyweight to never turn pro. "What is one million dollars, compared to the love of eight million Cubans?" he once said.

Cuba had every reason to love Stevenson. He dominated the heavyweight division for three Olympics, becoming the first boxer to win three gold medals in the same weight class. As of 2011, he was one of just three boxers to have won three gold medals at the Games.

Stevenson burst onto the scene in 1972 in Munich, West Germany. Early in the tournament, he defeated American Duane Bobick. Some people considered the win an upset since Bobick had defeated Stevenson a year earlier in the Pan-American Games. But it was no fluke. Using his powerful right hand, Stevenson cruised through the Games. It wasn't until the semifinals of the 1980 Olympics in Moscow, Soviet Union, that an Olympic opponent went the distance—three rounds—with Stevenson. In 1976 in Montreal, Quebec, Mircea Simion of Romania ran around the ring and tried to avoid the 6-foot-3 and 209-pound Stevenson for 2 rounds. But once Simion was hit in the third round, his coach threw in the towel and stopped the fight. "I have never been hit so hard in all my 212 bouts," said West Germany's Peter Hussing, who lost to Stevenson in the 1972 semifinals. "You don't see his right hand. All of a sudden it's there—on your chin."

Many people believe Stevenson would easily have won a fourth gold medal had Cuba not **boycotted** the 1984 Olympics in Los Angeles, California. (The communist Soviet Union chose not to compete in the Games that year in protest of American political policies, and 13 of its allies, including Cuba, joined the boycott.) After all, in 1986, when he was 34 years old, Stevenson showed he was still the best amateur heavyweight by winning at the World Amateur Boxing Championships in Reno, Nevada.

ATHENS, GREECE	PARIS, FRANCE	ST. LOUIS, MISSOURI	LONDON, ENGLAND	STOCKHOLM, SWEDEN	ANTWERP, BELGIUM	PARIS, FRANCE	AMSTERDAM, NETHERLANDS	LOS ANGELES, CALIFORNIA	BERLIN, GERMANY	LONDON, ENGLAND	HELSINKI, FINLAND	MELBOURNE, AUSTRALIA	ROME, ITALY	TOKYO, JAPAN	MEXICO CITY, MEXICO	MUNICH, WEST GERMANY	MONTREAL, QUEBEC	MOSCOW, SOVIET UNION	LOS ANGELES, CALIFORNIA	SEOUL, SOUTH KOREA	BARCELONA, SPAIN	ATLANTA, GEORGIA	SYDNEY, AUSTRALIA	ATHENS, GREECE	BEIJING, CHINA	LONDON, ENGLAND
1896	1900	1904	1908	1912	1920	1924	1928	1932	1936	1948	1952	1956	1960	1964	1968	1972	1976	1980	1984	1988	1992	1996	2000	2004	2008	2012

THE SPIRIT OF '76

1976 MONTREAL, QUEBEC

When the 1976 Olympics began in Montreal, Quebec, America's boxing team was full of unknown fighters. They were young and inexperienced, especially when compared with the Olympic favorites, who included veteran boxers from communist countries that did not allow them to become professionals. "We knew what we were up against—maturity and experience," said Pat Nappi, one

Famed for his speed, light-welterweight "Sugar" Ray Leonard (right) won 36 of his 40 lifetime fights

of the U.S. coaches. "Our kids would be out-experienced 10 to 1."

By the end of the Games, though, the Americans had become a famous group—and a winning one. They captured five gold medals, more than their country had won in the previous three Olympics combined and the most since five Americans won gold in the 1952 Olympics in Helsinki. Two other U.S. fighters left Montreal with medals, too.

Two of the gold medalists were brothers, Leon and Michael Spinks. Both would go on to have great success as professionals, winning heavyweight championships. In Montreal, Michael was a middleweight, and the older Leon was a light-heavyweight. The 23-year-old Leon, a Marine lance corporal, watched his little brother fight for the gold before he went into the ring. "I wanted him to win more than I wanted me to win," Leon said. Michael defeated the Soviet Union's Rufat Riskiyev by TKO at 1:54 of the third round. Leon likewise TKO'd world champion Sixto Soria of Cuba, as the referee stopped the fight just 69 seconds into the third round. It was the first time two brothers had won gold medals in boxing.

"Sugar" Ray Leonard breezed through the competition to win his gold medal. Despite boxing with sore hands, Leonard won all 6 of his Olympic light-welterweight bouts with unanimous, 5–0 decisions. In the finals, Leonard fought with photographs of his girlfriend and young son pinned to his socks. He defeated Cuba's Andrés Aldama, a boxer who would win gold at the 1980 Olympics in Moscow, Soviet Union. "My journey has ended," Leonard said afterward, announcing that he would be retiring from boxing and not turning pro. "My dream is fulfilled." Sugar Ray's retirement didn't last long, though, and he went on to a long career in which he won professional titles in five different weight classes.

In the lightweight division, Howard Davis Jr. used his skill and speed to take gold over Romania's Simion Cutov. He fought with a heavy heart, as his mother had died just two days before the Olympics began. "I dedicate this gold medal to my mother, wherever she may be," he said. Leo Randolph won the flyweight division, edging Cuba's Ramón Duvalón in a split decision.

Other U.S. medalists in Montreal were Charlie Mooney, who took silver in the bantamweight division, and Johnny Tate, who captured bronze at heavyweight. Tate lost in the semifinals to the great Cuban Teófilo Stevenson.

After his Olympic triumph, Leonard became a pro widely regarded as the best boxer of the 1980s

ATHENS, GREECE | 1896
PARIS, FRANCE | 1900
ST. LOUIS, MISSOURI | 1904
LONDON, ENGLAND | 1908
STOCKHOLM, SWEDEN | 1912
ANTWERP, BELGIUM | 1920
PARIS, FRANCE | 1924
AMSTERDAM, NETHERLANDS | 1928
LOS ANGELES, CALIFORNIA | 1932
BERLIN, GERMANY | 1936
LONDON, ENGLAND | 1948
HELSINKI, FINLAND | 1952
MELBOURNE, AUSTRALIA | 1956
ROME, ITALY | 1960
TOKYO, JAPAN | 1964
MEXICO CITY, MEXICO | 1968
MUNICH, WEST GERMANY | 1972
MONTREAL, QUEBEC | 1976
MOSCOW, SOVIET UNION | 1980
LOS ANGELES, CALIFORNIA | **1984**
SEOUL, SOUTH KOREA | 1988
BARCELONA, SPAIN | 1992
ATLANTA, GEORGIA | 1996
SYDNEY, AUSTRALIA | 2000
ATHENS, GREECE | 2004
BEIJING, CHINA | 2008
LONDON, ENGLAND | 2012

REAL DEAL, REAL WINNER

1984 LOS ANGELES, CALIFORNIA

When 21-year-old Evander Holyfield made his Olympic debut in 1984 in Los Angeles, California, not much was known about him. But it didn't take long for folks to start learning who he was. An American from Atlanta, Georgia, Holyfield introduced himself to the world's light-heavyweights in a series of short but memorable meetings in the ring.

Although dejected by his Olympic experience, Evander Holyfield went on to a three-decade pro career

The referee had to stop Holyfield's first two fights early, and in the quarterfinals, he knocked out Kenya's Sylvanus Okello with three seconds left in the first round. In the semifinals, Holyfield faced Kevin Barry of New Zealand. As he had in his first three bouts, Holyfield dominated Barry. Late in the second round, Holyfield put together a combination that ended with a vicious left hook to the side of the head that crumpled Barry. It was a knockout blow with five seconds left in the round.

But somewhere amid that flurry of punches—before the big left hook—referee Gligorije Novicic called on Holyfield to stop so he could break the two fighters apart. (Referees often move boxers back when they get tied up with each other, and Barry had begun holding the back of Holyfield's head.) Holyfield never had time to pull his punch, but the referee thought otherwise and disqualified him once it was determined that Barry was unfit to go on. Barry got the win, but because he had been knocked out, he would not be allowed to fight in the gold-medal match. That meant that Anton Josipovic of Yugoslavia would be awarded the top medal without having to box for it.

Both Barry and Josipovic knew who should have won the gold—Holyfield, who was nicknamed "The Real Deal." After Novicic took both Barry and Holyfield to the center of the ring and raised Barry's hand as the winner of their fight, Barry grabbed Holyfield's hand and raised it up to show who he thought had won the fight. Immediately, a chorus of boos echoed through the Los Angeles Memorial Sports Arena. Later, after Josipovic was given the gold medal and the Yugoslavian national anthem was played, he shook Holyfield's hand and pulled him up to the top **podium** from the bronze-medal position.

Historically formidable boxing countries such as the Soviet Union, Cuba, and other communist nations boycotted the 1984 Olympics. As a result, the U.S. dominated the boxing competition, winning nine gold medals and one silver. But it was Holyfield's bronze that boxing fans most remember. "It made me more popular than all the other guys that won the gold medal," Holyfield said. Holyfield went on to great success as a professional fighter, winning the heavyweight championship of the world four times.

ATHENS, GREECE 1896
PARIS, FRANCE 1900
ST. LOUIS, MISSOURI 1904
LONDON, ENGLAND 1908
STOCKHOLM, SWEDEN 1912
ANTWERP, BELGIUM 1920
PARIS, FRANCE 1924
AMSTERDAM, NETHERLANDS 1928
LOS ANGELES, CALIFORNIA 1932
BERLIN, GERMANY 1936
LONDON, ENGLAND 1948
HELSINKI, FINLAND 1952
MELBOURNE, AUSTRALIA 1956
ROME, ITALY 1960
TOKYO, JAPAN 1964
MEXICO CITY, MEXICO 1968
MUNICH, WEST GERMANY 1972
MONTREAL, QUEBEC 1976
MOSCOW, SOVIET UNION 1980
LOS ANGELES, CALIFORNIA 1984
SEOUL, SOUTH KOREA 1988
BARCELONA, SPAIN 1992
ATLANTA, GEORGIA 1996
SYDNEY, AUSTRALIA 2000
ATHENS, GREECE 2004
BEIJING, CHINA 2008
LONDON, ENGLAND 2012

ROBBED OF GOLD

1988 SEOUL, SOUTH KOREA

If a boxer doesn't win by KO or TKO, the decision on who wins and who loses comes down to five judges watching the bout at the side of the ring. In Olympic boxing, the judges' job is to keep track of the blows that each fighter lands on the other's head or body. Each punch earns the

The 1988 scandal left Roy Jones Jr. (left) stunned, the referee disgusted, and Park Si-Hun (right) embarrassed

fighter a point, and whoever scores the most points wins the fight. It's not a perfect system, though. Human error and even cheating and corruption can easily change gold into silver. That's what happened to American Roy Jones Jr. in 1988 in Seoul, South Korea.

In the light-middleweight division's championship bout, Jones faced South Korea's Park Si-Hun. Park had an arena full of people cheering him, hoping he'd win a gold medal for the host country. Jones had dominated the competition leading up to the finals, scoring a KO and three consecutive unanimous decisions. He was riding high and all set to pummel Park in front of the Korean fans.

That's just what Jones did. He landed blow after blow for 3 rounds, outscoring Park 20–3 in the first round, 30–15 in the second, and 36–14 in the third. Jones even forced a standing-eight count (a rule that allows the referee to briefly stop the fight and determine whether a battered fighter can continue) of Park in the second round. It was plain to the television commentators and the millions of fans watching on TV that Jones had dominated the match.

Then the judges' scores came in. Two judges said Jones had won a close fight. Two others said Park had won. The fifth judge scored it a draw, but he ruled that Park was the more aggressive fighter and so gave the point to the Korean. While the Korean crowd cheered, Jones cried in the corner of the ring. Americans were outraged by the result, and Park was embarrassed by his "victory." "I am sorry," he told Jones. "I lost the fight. I feel very bad."

The judges were accused of taking bribes from Korean officials. One of the judges admitted that he made a mistake. "The American won easily—so easily, in fact, that I was positive my four fellow judges would score the fight for the American by a wide margin," Moroccan judge Hiduad Larbi said. "So I voted for the Korean to make the score only 4–1 for the American and not embarrass the host country."

While Jones never received the gold medal he deserved, he was awarded the Val Barker Trophy, and the three judges who voted against him were suspended. The scandal also compelled Olympic officials to change the way bouts were scored after that, going to an electronic system in which judges push a button to record each punch they see land.

ATHENS, GREECE	PARIS, FRANCE	ST. LOUIS, MISSOURI	LONDON, ENGLAND	STOCKHOLM, SWEDEN	ANTWERP, BELGIUM	PARIS, FRANCE	AMSTERDAM, NETHERLANDS	LOS ANGELES, CALIFORNIA	BERLIN, GERMANY	LONDON, ENGLAND	HELSINKI, FINLAND	MELBOURNE, AUSTRALIA	ROME, ITALY	TOKYO, JAPAN	MEXICO CITY, MEXICO	MUNICH, WEST GERMANY	MONTREAL, QUEBEC	MOSCOW, SOVIET UNION	LOS ANGELES, CALIFORNIA	SEOUL, SOUTH KOREA	BARCELONA, SPAIN	ATLANTA, GEORGIA	SYDNEY, AUSTRALIA	ATHENS, GREECE	BEIJING, CHINA	LONDON, ENGLAND
1896	1900	1904	1908	1912	1920	1924	1928	1932	1936	1948	1952	1956	1960	1964	1968	1972	1976	1980	1984	1988	**1992**	1996	2000	2004	2008	2012

KEEPING HIS PROMISE

OSCAR DE LA HOYA U.S. WEIGHT CLASS: LIGHTWEIGHT

OLYMPIC COMPETITION: 1992

Two years before the 1992 Olympics took place in Barcelona, Spain, Oscar De La Hoya's mother, Cecilia, was dying of cancer. Oscar was an up-and-coming fighter, and Cecilia told her son that her dying wish was for him to win the Olympic gold medal. Oscar told her he'd do it for her.

Oscar De La Hoya used his mother, country, and heritage as motivation during his 1992 run to glory

36

"That is my motivation," De La Hoya said before traveling to Spain as the U.S.'s best lightweight fighter two years later. "To win the gold, it has to come from your heart."

De La Hoya dominated his first three matches. In the first fight, Brazil's Adilson Silva opened a cut below De La Hoya's left eye, but that didn't bother the American. By the third round, De La Hoya was the one doing the damage and scoring points with jabs, hooks, and uppercuts. With seven seconds left in the match, the referee stopped the fight. De La Hoya easily won his next two matches on points to advance to the semifinals, where he faced Hong Seong-Sik of South Korea.

De La Hoya had to win the semifinal match in order to get the chance to keep his promise. "There's a lot of pressure when you're favored to win the gold," the American said. "Some guys are coming into this with nothing to lose. They're just here for respect. But the pressure is on me. I'm expected to win." De La Hoya trailed after the first round but eventually squeaked out an 11 – 10 decision. (A new scoring system had been put in place after the controversy in the 1988 Games.)

Awaiting De La Hoya in the finals was Germany's Marco Rudolph. This would be no easy match. Rudolph was the world's reigning lightweight amateur champion, and he had defeated De La Hoya for that title a year earlier. The two boxers were tied after the first round, and De La Hoya had a slim, one-point lead after the second. But there was no doubt about the third. De La Hoya knocked Rudolph down with a left hook and eventually won the match on points, 7 – 2. "That was probably his best fight of the whole tournament," said U.S. coach Joe Byrd.

De La Hoya, who would become known as "The Golden Boy" after the Olympics, was the only American boxer to win a gold medal in 1992. Had he not won, it would have been the first time the U.S. had failed to win a gold medal in the sport since 1948. After the bout, De La Hoya, a native of Los Angeles, California, waved two flags—one American and one Mexican. The Mexican flag was in honor of his parents, who were born in Mexico. Oscar's mother's wish was granted. "Mission accomplished," he said.

"To win the gold, it has to come from your heart." – *Oscar De La Hoya*

1896	1900	1904	1908	1912	1920	1924	1928	1932	1936	1948	1952	1956	1960	1964	1968	1972	1976	1980	1984	1988	1992	1996	2000	2004	2008	2012
ATHENS, GREECE	PARIS, FRANCE	ST. LOUIS, MISSOURI	LONDON, ENGLAND	STOCKHOLM, SWEDEN	ANTWERP, BELGIUM	PARIS, FRANCE	AMSTERDAM, NETHERLANDS	LOS ANGELES, CALIFORNIA	BERLIN, GERMANY	LONDON, ENGLAND	HELSINKI, FINLAND	MELBOURNE, AUSTRALIA	ROME, ITALY	TOKYO, JAPAN	MEXICO CITY, MEXICO	MUNICH, WEST GERMANY	MONTREAL, QUEBEC	MOSCOW, SOVIET UNION	LOS ANGELES, CALIFORNIA	SEOUL, SOUTH KOREA	BARCELONA, SPAIN	ATLANTA, GEORGIA	SYDNEY, AUSTRALIA	ATHENS, GREECE	BEIJING, CHINA	LONDON, ENGLAND

HEIR TO STEVENSON

FÉLIX SAVÓN   CUBA   WEIGHT CLASS: HEAVYWEIGHT

OLYMPIC COMPETITIONS: 1992, 1996, 2000

After Teófilo Stevenson won his third gold medal in 1980 in Moscow, Soviet Union, his home country of Cuba boycotted the next two Olympics. The country chose not to participate in the Olympics in 1984 or 1988 to protest the political policies of the host countries, America and South Korea. That ended

Félix Savón was considered a Cuban national treasure and was a favorite of president Fidel Castro

39

Savón's 2000 gold medal was his last triumph, but he helped train Cuba's boxers for the 2004 Games

Stevenson's reign over the heavyweight division. But when Cuba returned to the Games in 1992 in Barcelona, Spain, a new one-man dynasty was about to begin.

Félix Savón was Cuba's newest phenomenon, and he picked up where Stevenson had left off. Standing 6-foot-6, Savón was an intimidating figure. He reminded his foes of his height advantage each time he entered the ring by stepping over the ropes rather than dipping between them. In Spain, the 24-year-old struggled through a quarterfinal match against American Danell Nicholson, coming from behind to win by just 2 points. But he rolled to the gold from there, dominating his next two opponents 23–3 and 14–1. "He's the Olympic champion," Stevenson said after Savón defeated Nigeria's David Izon in the 1992 final match. "Three times I was the Olympic heavyweight champion. He fought very well and now he is the best." Stevenson claimed that Savón was even better than he was. However, Savón was still two gold medals shy of matching his countryman at the time.

Sure enough, Félix caught up with his legendary **predecessor**. He crushed Canada's David Defiagbon during the gold-medal match in 1996 in Atlanta, Georgia. In 2000 in Sydney, Australia, he defeated Russia's Sultan Ibragimov for his third gold and retired shortly after that.

Savón dominated the amateur heavyweight division in international boxing for 14 years, winning 6 world titles along with his 3 Olympic golds. Many experts believe he would have begun his streak earlier and earned four gold medals had Cuba chosen to participate in the 1988 Games. But Savón stayed true to his country. Even though Cuba's communist government did not allow him to leave the country to turn pro as so many American fighters had done following their Olympic experiences, Savón said he wouldn't have wanted to have boxed for money. "I don't like professional boxing," he said. "I like boxing but only as a pastime, as a sport, as leisure. That's the only reason I box."

Savón never sought the money or publicity of pro boxing, once calling it "a very dirty sport"

1896	1900	1904	1908	1912	1920	1924	1928	1932	1936	1948	1952	1956	1960	1964	1968	1972	1976	1980	1984	1988	1992	1996	2000	2004	2008	**2012**
ATHENS, GREECE	PARIS, FRANCE	ST. LOUIS, MISSOURI	LONDON, ENGLAND	STOCKHOLM, SWEDEN	ANTWERP, BELGIUM	PARIS, FRANCE	AMSTERDAM, NETHERLANDS	LOS ANGELES, CALIFORNIA	BERLIN, GERMANY	LONDON, ENGLAND	HELSINKI, FINLAND	MELBOURNE, AUSTRALIA	ROME, ITALY	TOKYO, JAPAN	MEXICO CITY, MEXICO	MUNICH, WEST GERMANY	MONTREAL, QUEBEC	MOSCOW, SOVIET UNION	LOS ANGELES, CALIFORNIA	SEOUL, SOUTH KOREA	BARCELONA, SPAIN	ATLANTA, GEORGIA	SYDNEY, AUSTRALIA	ATHENS, GREECE	BEIJING, CHINA	**LONDON, ENGLAND**

THE GAMES OF 2012

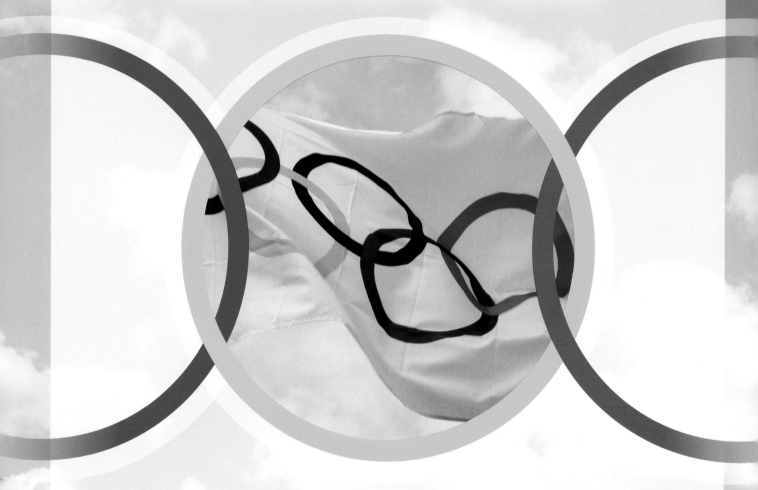

The 2012 Olympics were to be held in London, England. Londoners got the news in July 2005, and as is the case any time an Olympic host is selected, city and national officials sprang into action. Although seven years may seem to be plenty of time for preparation, it is in fact a small window when one considers that host cities typically need to create housing for thousands of

In 2012, London was to play host to its third Summer Olympiad, having done so in 1908 and 1948

international athletes and coaches (generally in a consolidated area known as the "Athletes' Village"), expand public transportation options (such as trains and buses), and build outdoor playing fields, indoor arenas, and other venues with enough seating—and grandeur—to be worthy of Olympic competition.

The numbers involved in the 2012 Games indicate just how large a venture it is to host an Olympiad. Some 10,500 athletes from 200 countries were to compete in London, with 2,100 medals awarded. About 8 million tickets were expected to be sold for the Games. And before any athletes arrived or any medals were awarded, it was anticipated that the total cost of London's Olympics-related building projects and other preparations would approach $15 billion.

Among those construction projects was the creation of Olympic Park, a sprawling gathering area in east London that was to function as a center of activity during the Games. From the park, people would be able to move to numerous athletic facilities in and around the city. Those facilities included the 80,000-seat Olympic Stadium, which was built to host track

and field events as well as the opening and closing ceremonies; the new Basketball Arena, a temporary structure that was to be dismantled after the Games; and the $442-million Aquatics Centre, which was designed both to host swimming events and to serve as a kind of visitors' gateway to Olympic Park. Other notable venues included the North Greenwich Arena (which was to host gymnastics), the ExCeL center (boxing), Earls Court (indoor volleyball), and Horse Guards Parade (beach volleyball).

In July 2011, British prime minister David Cameron and IOC president Jacques Rogge reviewed all preparations and proudly declared that the city was nearly ready to welcome the world. "This has the makings of a great British success story," Cameron announced. "With a year to go, it's on time, it's on budget…. We must offer the greatest ever Games in the world's greatest country."

Rogge kicked off the one-year countdown to the Games by formally inviting countries around the world to send their greatest athletes to the British capital in 2012. "The athletes will be ready," said Rogge. "And so will London."

amateur — not a professional; boxers who compete professionally (for pay) are barred from Olympic competition

ambassadors — people who represent a country or government or serve to deliver a message or goodwill to another nation

binge — to do too much of something in a short amount of time, usually with negative consequences

boycotted — protested or showed disapproval of something by refusing to participate in an event

bribes — money or other valuables given in return for favors or services; often the exchanges are for something illegal or dishonest

combinations — in boxing, series of punches landed on an opponent over short periods of time

communist — describing a government that has tight control over a country's resources and people; many communist countries were rivals of the U.S. from the 1940s to the 1990s

corner — in boxing, the people who assist a fighter before and after the match and between rounds; the group may include a coach, a trainer, and a cut man (whose job is to make quick repairs to cuts)

decision — in boxing, the outcome of a match in which neither fighter is knocked out and judges decide the winner based on points; a decision may either be split (with judges disagreeing) or unanimous (with all judges agreeing)

draw — in sports, a tie game or match

dregs — the worst or most useless parts of something

hook — a short but powerful punch that is delivered sideways with a bent arm

jab — a short, quick, straight punch

podium — a raised platform; in the Olympics, the top three finishers stand atop podiums of varying heights to receive their medals

predecessor — a person who comes before another in time, especially in the same job or sport

round — one section of a boxing match, begun and ended with the ringing of a bell; Olympic matches currently consist of four 2-minute rounds (in the past, they consisted of three 3-minute rounds)

single-elimination — a tournament format in which a loss eliminates an athlete or team from the competition

southpaw — a person who is left-handed; the term is often used to describe left-handed athletes, especially boxers and baseball pitchers

sparring — boxing practice

uppercuts — swinging punches that are delivered upward, usually to an opponent's chin

Val Barker Trophy — an award given to the most outstanding and stylistic boxer of an Olympic Games; the trophy honors Val Barker, a successful British heavyweight of the late 1800s and early 1900s

weight classes — levels of competition based on a boxer's weight; Olympic weight classes have varied over the years but as of 2012 included flyweight (112 pounds), bantamweight (119), featherweight (126), lightweight (132), light-welterweight (141), welterweight (152), middleweight (165), light-heavyweight (179), heavyweight (201), and super-heavyweight (202 and up)

Selected Bibliography

Cousineau, Phil. *The Olympic Odyssey: Rekindling the True Spirit of the Great Games.* Wheaton, Ill.: The Theosophical Publishing House, 2003.

Levy, Alan Howard. *Floyd Patterson: A Boxer and a Gentleman.* Jefferson, N.C.: McFarland & Company, 2008.

MacCambridge, Michael, ed. *SportsCentury.* New York: ESPN, 1999.

Macy, Sue, and Bob Costas. *Swifter, Higher, Stronger: A Photographic History of the Summer Olympics.* Washington, D.C.: National Geographic, 2008.

Maraniss, David. Rome *1960: The Olympics that Changed the World.* New York: Simon & Schuster, 2008.

Nack, William. "Slight Heavies." *Sports Illustrated,* August 17, 1992.

Putnam, Pat. "Travesty." *Sports Illustrated,* October 10, 1988.

Wilbon, Michael. "De La Hoya Fights Way to Gold." *The Washington Post,* August 9, 1992.

Web Sites

International Olympic Committee
www.olympic.org
This site is the official online home of the Olympics and features profiles of athletes, overviews of every sport, coverage of preparation for the 2012 Summer Games, and more.

Sports-Reference / Olympic Sports
www.sports-reference.com/olympics
This site is a comprehensive database for Olympic sports and features complete facts and statistics from all Olympic Games, including medal counts, Olympic records, and more.

INDEX

Published by Creative Education
P.O. Box 227, Mankato, Minnesota 56002
Creative Education is an imprint of
The Creative Company
www.thecreativecompany.us

Design and production by The Design Lab
Art direction by Rita Marshall

Printed by Corporate Graphics in
the United States of America

Photographs by Alamy (Everett Collection
Inc), American Numismatic Society, Corbis
(Bettmann), Dreamstime (Albo, Alain Lacroix,
Mikhail Popov), Getty Images (AFP, Al Bello/
ALLSPORT, Al Bello, Stephen Dunn /Allsport,
Focus on Sport/Getty Images, Haynes Archive/
Popperfoto, John Iacono /Sports Illustrated,
Marc Morrison /Allsport, Marvin E. Newman /
Sports Illustrated, Hank Olen/NY Daily News
Archive, Popperfoto, Mike Powell /Allsport,
SSPL, STAFF/AFP, STF/AFP, Billy Stickland,
Bob Thomas), iStockphoto (ray roper), Library
of Congress, Prints & Photographs Division
(LC-DIG-ggbain-11104)

Library of Congress
Cataloging-in-Publication Data
Frederick, Shane.
Boxing / by Shane Frederick.
p. cm. — (Summer Olympic legends)
Summary: A survey of the highlights and
legendary athletes—such as Cuban Teófilo
Stevenson—of the Olympic sport of boxing,
which officially became a part of the modern
Summer Games in 1904.
Includes bibliographical references and index.
ISBN 978-1-60818-209-1
1. Boxers (Sports)—Biography—Juvenile literature.
2. Boxing—Juvenile literature. 3. Olympics—
Juvenile literature. I. Title.
GV 1131.F84 2012
796.83—dc23   2011032495

CPSIA: 070212 PO1591

9 8 7 6 5 4 3 2